I0751498

BUILT ON PURPOSE

A BLUEPRINT FOR FORMING MISSIONAL TEAMS

Jacob Abshire

Built on Purpose: A Blueprint for Forming Missional Teams

7010 Turtle Manor Dr, Humble, TX 77346
www.JacobAbshire.com

Design and typeset: Resolute Creative, Inc., Houston, TX
Printed in the United States of America

ISBN: 000
Kindle ISBN: 000
ePub ISBN: 000
Nook ISBN: 000

Dedicated to the founding members of Devo Church (Houston, TX) who patiently and faithfully devoted themselves to mission of God.

CONTENTS

9THE PROJECT

The first time on a construction site can be daunting. At first glance, it might look messy—materials scattered, tools everywhere, pieces that don't seem to fit together. But what you don't see at first is how the blueprint brings it all together. The builder knows exactly what he is doing. Every beam, every measurement, every placement is intentional. Nothing is random.

In the same way, your life can feel like a collection of disconnected experiences of successes, failures, relationships, and opportunities. But God is the builder, and He is working from a perfect design. This guide will help you step back and see the blueprint. It will help you get a vision of how He has formed you, where you fit, and how He is building something powerful through your team.

GOD IS THE BUILDER. THIS PROCESS HELPS YOU SEE THE BLUEPRINT.

A NOTE TO PARTICIPANTS

Before anything is built through us, something must be formed within us. The Lord does not simply use people—He shapes them. He prepares hearts, clarifies calling, strengthens conviction, and knits people together for His purposes. This guide will help you submit yourself to the work of God in your life.

As you walk through this process, come with humility and honesty. Be willing to reflect deeply, to speak openly, and to listen carefully. The goal is not perfection, but clarity—seeing how God has been at work in you and how He is leading you forward.

At the same time, this is not an individual journey alone. God forms His people in community. As you share with one another, you will begin to see how your lives, gifts, and callings fit together for something greater than any one person.

Above all, remember that Christ is the builder of His church. We are not creating something new—we are participating in what He is already doing. Trust Him in the process. Be faithful in what is in front of you. And allow Him to shape you, both personally and together, for the work He has prepared.

In short, this guide is designed to cultivate thoughtful, self-aware, and mission-minded leaders by guiding them to reflect deeply on Scripture, their own lives, and their relationships—so the team can discern how God has shaped each member for the building of His church.

HOW THE GUIDE WORKS

This guide contains twelve exercises designed to help form and prepare a team for the work of ministry. These exercises are typically paired together to create a six-week process, though they may also be completed individually over twelve weeks.

(The more lengthy timespan is recommended.) Each exercise includes a short biblical lesson, a guided reflection, and a focused writing assignment.

Participants are expected to complete each exercise individually throughout the week. While these reflections are personal, participants are encouraged to share and process them with a spouse when appropriate. Each exercise is designed to move from contemplation to clarity, requiring thoughtful writing and a final one-sentence summary.

Leaders should teach the corresponding lesson prior to assigning each exercise. In a weekly format, this means the lesson is taught one week, and the exercise is completed in the days that follow. Participants are encouraged to keep a journal as they work through the process, as some exercises may also include reading, assessments, or additional reflection.

When the group gathers, participants will discuss their reflections together under the guidance of a leader. These discussions are essential—they help the team grow in understanding one another and discerning how God has uniquely shaped each person. Leaders should take notes or assign someone to do so, as these insights will be valuable for future direction and team development.

USING THE EXERCISES

It is recommended that you spend one week on each exercise. After the corresponding lesson is taught, take time the next day to revisit the lesson and record key insights in a journal. Then, begin a simple list of thoughts prompted by the exercise—initial reflections, memories, questions, and ideas.

Over the next couple of days, return to that list and refine it. Add new insights, remove what feels unnecessary, and begin to notice patterns. This slower process is intentional—it allows you to think more clearly and reflect more deeply rather than rushing to a response.

Around day four or five, write out your reflection in paragraph form according to the instructions. Then, on day six, reduce your thoughts to a single sentence that captures the essence of what you've discovered. This process helps move you from awareness to clarity, preparing you to contribute meaningfully in group discussion and helping others better understand how God has shaped your life.

INTRODUCTION

MATTHEW 4:18-22

Jesus intentionally calls, forms, and sends ordinary people into His mission. In Matthew 4, we see the beginning of Jesus' public ministry and the formation of His team. He does not begin with crowds, systems, or structures—He begins with people. These first disciples are not religious elites or proven leaders; they are ordinary men in the middle of their daily lives. This passage gives us a clear picture of how Jesus builds His team and prepares them for the work ahead.

First, Jesus calls people personally. As He walks by the Sea of Galilee, He sees Simon Peter and Andrew casting their nets and says, "Follow me" (Matt. 4:18–20). This call is direct and relational. Before it is about what they will do, it is about who they will be with. Jesus does not recruit them based on their qualifications—He invites them into a relationship. This reminds us that ministry begins with being with Christ before doing anything for Him. How might your approach to ministry change if you prioritized being with Jesus over working for Him?

Second, Jesus reorients their purpose. He says, "I will make you fishers of men" (Matt. 4:19). These men were already fishermen, but Jesus transformed their identity and direction. He takes what they know and redirects it toward His mission. This shows that calling is not about abandoning who you are, but about being reshaped for God's purposes. Jesus forms His disciples over time, aligning their lives with His work. In what ways might God be redirecting what you already do toward His mission?

Third, Jesus forms a team, not individuals. He calls Peter and Andrew, and then James and John shortly after (Matt. 4:21–22). From the beginning, Jesus is building a group, not just developing isolated followers. The Christian life is not meant to be lived alone, and ministry is not meant to be carried out individually. Jesus creates a community that will grow, learn, and be sent together. What does it look like for you to not only follow Jesus personally, but to be formed alongside others?

As we begin this process, it is important to see that we are stepping into the same pattern. Jesus calls us personally, reshapes our purpose, and places us within a team for His mission. This is not just training—it is a formation process. He is building His church by forming His people, and we are part of that work.

FOUNDATION STAGE

WHO HAS GOD MADE YOU TO BE?

Every structure rises or falls on its foundation. Before anything is framed, shaped, or built upward, the foundation must be carefully laid. It is unseen once the structure is complete, but it determines everything—its strength, its stability, and its longevity.

In the same way, God does not begin His work in us with outward activity, but with inward formation. He establishes who we are before He directs what we do. This section is about stepping back to see the foundation God has already laid in your life—how He has formed you, where He has been at work, and what He is building beneath the surface.

Scripture consistently shows that God's work begins with identity before function. Before the disciples were sent, they were called. Before they were given a mission, they were brought into a relationship with Christ.

In this section, you will explore two foundational realities: *your journey* and *your calling*. Your journey helps you trace the hand of God in your life—how He has formed and prepared you. Your calling helps you discern how that formation connects to His purposes moving forward. Together, these lessons will help you see that your life is not random, but intentionally built by God for His work.

STEP 1:

YOUR JOURNEY

PSALM 139:13-14

God has intentionally formed every part of your life for His purposes. Psalm 139 is David's reflection on the intimate knowledge and intentional design of God over his life. He is not merely acknowledging that God knows him, but that God has actively shaped him—before birth, through life, and into the future. This passage gives us a framework to understand that our story is not accidental but authored. As we begin to reflect on our journey, we are not just remembering events—we are tracing the hand of God.

First, God forms you personally. David says, "You formed my inward parts; you knitted me together in my mother's womb" (Ps. 139:13). This speaks to intentional design. Your personality, your wiring, your natural tendencies—these are not random traits but crafted by God. Even the parts of you that you may not fully understand or even like were formed with purpose. This means your life did not begin when you became aware of God—it began with God's deliberate involvement. How might your view of yourself change if you truly believed that God designed you on purpose?

Second, God sees your whole story. David continues, "My frame was not hidden from you… when I was being made in secret" (Ps. 139:15). God's knowledge of you is not partial—it is complete. He has seen every season, every hardship, every moment of growth and failure. Nothing in your life has been overlooked or wasted. The experiences that have shaped you—both joyful and painful—are all within God's sight and sovereignty. This means your past is not something to hide from but something to understand in light of God's work. Where have you seen God's hand most clearly in your story, even if you didn't recognize it at the time?

Third, God ordains your days. David concludes, "In your book were written… the days that were formed for me" (Ps. 139:16). Not only has God formed you and seen you, but He has also ordered your life. Your timeline, your opportunities, your limitations—these are all part of His design. This does not remove responsibility, but it does give meaning. God has been preparing you, shaping you, and positioning you for His purposes. Your life is not a collection of disconnected moments—it is a story moving toward His mission. How might your perspective shift if you saw your life as preparation rather than coincidence?

As you reflect on your journey, begin to see your life through this lens: formed by God, seen by God, and directed by God. This means your story matters—not just to you, but to the mission of God through His church. Understanding your journey helps others understand how God has shaped you for the work ahead.

GOD HAS BEEN PREPARING YOU, SHAPING YOU, AND POSITIONING YOU FOR HIS PURPOSES.

EXERCISE

On one page, write the story of your life with a focus on how God has shaped you. Consider key moments such as your upbringing, your salvation, seasons of growth, hardships, relationships, and experiences that have influenced who you are today. As you write, ask yourself: Where do I see God forming me? What experiences have most shaped my character? What moments strengthened or challenged my faith?

After writing your full reflection, identify one area where you sense a need for growth moving forward. Then, reduce your entire reflection to one clear sentence that captures how God has shaped you and where He is leading you next. Be prepared to share both your story and your sentence in the next gathering.

Reflections:

One-Sentence Summary:

STEP 2:

YOUR CALLING

EPHESIANS 2:8-10

You are saved and shaped by grace and sent with purpose. In Ephesians 2, Paul reminds believers of the foundation of their salvation and the direction of their lives. These verses move from what God has *done for us* to what God has *designed for us*. Calling is not something we create for ourselves—it is something we discover in light of God's grace and God's work. Before we think about roles, positions, or ambitions, we must first understand that calling begins with God.

First, you are saved by grace, not by performance. Paul writes, "For by grace you have been saved through faith… not a result of works" (Eph. 2:8–9). This means your identity is not built on what you do, but on what Christ has done. Calling does not begin with striving—it begins with resting in the finished work of Jesus. Many people confuse calling with pressure to prove themselves, but Scripture removes that burden. You are already accepted in Christ. How might your sense of calling change if it flowed from grace instead of performance?

Second, you are created for good works. Paul continues, "For we are his workmanship, created in Christ Jesus for good works" (Eph. 2:10). The word "workmanship" carries the idea of a crafted masterpiece. God has not only saved you—He is shaping you for specific works. These works align with your gifts, experiences, and opportunities. Your calling is often discovered at the intersection of how God has made you and where He has placed you. What kinds of opportunities or burdens seem to consistently draw your attention?

Third, your calling is prepared beforehand by God. Paul says these are works "which God prepared beforehand, that we should walk in them" (Eph. 2:10). This means your calling is not something you have to invent—it is something you step into. God has already gone before you, arranging opportunities for you to live out your faith. Your role is not to manufacture meaning, but to walk faithfully in what God places in front of you. Calling is less about finding a distant destination and more about faithfully responding to present opportunities. Where do you see God already opening doors in your life?

As you consider your calling, remember this: you are not trying to become someone else—you are learning to walk in what God has already designed for you. Your calling flows from grace, is shaped by your design, and is revealed through obedience. Understanding this will help you move forward with clarity and confidence in the mission of God.

**YOU ARE NOT CREATING YOUR CALLING–
YOU ARE DISCOVERING IT.**

EXERCISE

On one page, describe your sense of calling. Reflect on your ambitions, ideas, and the things you feel drawn toward. Consider what others have affirmed in you—what encouragements or patterns have people consistently pointed out? Think about your convictions—what burdens or passions has God placed on your heart? Also reflect on what you have to offer in God's kingdom, including your time, talents, resources, and spiritual gifts.

As you write, ask yourself: What do I feel compelled to do for God's kingdom? Where have others seen fruit in my life? What do I naturally gravitate toward? What do I have to invest? After completing your reflection, reduce everything to one sentence that clearly captures your sense of calling. Be prepared to share and discuss how your calling might connect with others on the team.

Reflections:

One-Sentence Summary:

FRAMING STAGE

HOW HAVE YOU BEEN SHAPED?

Once the foundation is laid, the next step is framing. This is where the structure begins to take visible shape. Walls go up, spaces are defined, and you can begin to see how everything will come together. Framing connects what is unseen to what will be experienced—it gives form to the structure.

In the same way, your life has been shaped over time through experiences, relationships, and environments. These moments have framed how you think, what you expect, and how you engage with others. This section helps you step back and examine how God has used your past to shape your present.

Scripture shows that God forms His people not only through direct instruction, but through lived experience. The early church did not develop in isolation—it was shaped through teaching, fellowship, challenges, and growth.

In this section, you will reflect on your *church experience* and your *discipleship experience.* Your church experience reveals how your expectations and perspectives have been formed, both positively and negatively. Your discipleship experience helps you see how you have been personally developed—and how you might develop others. Together, these lessons will help you recognize the framework God has been building in your life and how it influences the way you move forward.

STEP 3:

CHURCH EXPERIENCE

ACTS 2:42-47

God defines what the church should be, not our experiences. In Acts 2, we are given a clear picture of the early church immediately after the gospel takes root. This is not a perfect church, but it is a faithful one—devoted to Christ and shaped by His Word, His people, and His power. For many of us, our understanding of the church has been formed more by experience than by Scripture. This passage helps reorient us so that we evaluate the church not by preference or past wounds, but by God's design.

First, the church is devoted to the right things. Luke writes, "They devoted themselves to the apostles' teaching and the fellowship, to the breaking of bread and the prayers" (Acts 2:42). The defining mark of the church is not its programs or personality, but its devotion—especially to God's Word, God's people, and God's presence. This devotion is active and persistent. Many of our past experiences may have emphasized other things, but Scripture brings us back to what matters most. When you think about your past church experiences, what were they most devoted to?

Second, the church shares life together. The passage describes a people who were "together and had all things in common" (Acts 2:44), meeting needs, sharing meals, and living with gladness and sincerity (Acts 2:46). This is more than attendance—it is participation in a spiritual family. Some of us have experienced this kind of fellowship, while others have not. Our experiences may have included isolation, surface-level relationships, or even hurt. Yet this passage shows us what a true biblical community looks like. How have your past experiences shaped your expectations of relationships within the church?

Third, the church displays the power of God. Luke says they had "favor with all the people," and "the Lord added to their number day by day those who were being saved" (Acts 2:47). When the church is devoted to the right things and living in genuine community, God works through it. Growth, influence, and transformation are the result of God's activity, not human effort alone. This challenges us to evaluate whether our expectations of the church are shaped by God's power or by past disappointments. In what ways have your experiences either strengthened or weakened your expectation that God is at work in His church?

As you reflect on your church experience, allow Scripture to both affirm and correct your perspective. Your past matters—it has shaped you—but it does not define what the church is meant to be. God's Word does. Understanding this will help you move forward with clarity, humility, and hope as you engage in the life of the church.

SCRIPTURE DEFINES THE CHURCH, NOT OUR EXPERIENCES.

EXERCISE

On one page, describe your past church experiences—the good, the bad, and the challenging. Reflect on the environments you've been part of and how they have shaped your view of the church. Consider what you appreciated, what frustrated you, and what left a lasting impact on you.

As you write, ask yourself: What did I value most about my past church experiences? What disappointed or hurt me? How have these experiences shaped my expectations of church today? What do I wish was different? After completing your reflection, reduce your thoughts to one sentence that captures how your church experience has shaped you. Be prepared to share and discuss how your perspective may influence how you engage with this team and the church moving forward.

Reflections:

One-Sentence Summary:

STEP 4:

DISCIPLESHIP EXPERIENCE

2 TIMOTHY 2:1-2

Discipleship is intentional multiplication through faithful relationships. In 2 Timothy, Paul writes to Timothy near the end of his life, passing on what matters most. He does not simply give instruction—he gives a model. This passage shows us that discipleship is not accidental or informal alone; it is purposeful, relational, and generational. As we reflect on our own discipleship experience, we are not just asking what we received, but how it was passed on.

First, discipleship is strengthened by grace. Paul begins, "You then, my child, be strengthened by the grace that is in Christ Jesus" (2 Tim. 2:1). Before Timothy can disciple others, he must be rooted in Christ. Discipleship does not start with methods or systems—it starts with a life that is being sustained by grace. If someone discipled you well, they likely pointed you back to Christ, not just to habits or knowledge. And if that has been lacking, it reveals where discipleship must begin. Who or what has most shaped your dependence on Christ?

Second, discipleship is entrusted through relationships. Paul says, "What you have heard from me… entrust to faithful men" (2 Tim. 2:2). This is deeply relational language. Timothy did not just receive information from Paul—he shared life with him. Discipleship involves trust, proximity, and intentional investment. It is not merely teaching content, but transferring a way of life. Many people have sat under teaching, but fewer have experienced this kind of personal investment. Have you experienced someone intentionally pouring into you, or have you mostly learned from a distance?

Third, discipleship is designed for multiplication. Paul continues, "who will be able to teach others also" (2 Tim. 2:2). This creates four generations: Paul → Timothy → faithful men → others. True discipleship is not complete until it reproduces. It is not just about personal growth, but about equipping others to grow and lead. This means that even now, you are being prepared not only to receive discipleship but to give it. How has your past experience prepared you—or failed to prepare you—to disciple someone else?

As you reflect on your discipleship experience, consider both what you have received and what is still needed. Some have been deeply invested in, while others have not had that opportunity. Either way, this exercise helps us establish a shared understanding: discipleship is intentional, relational, and reproducible. This is the kind of culture we are building together.

**YOU ARE NOT ONLY CALLED TO GROW.
YOU ARE CALLED TO MULTIPLY.**

EXERCISE

On one page, describe your discipleship experience. If someone has discipled you, reflect on who they were and what they did. What stood out about the way they invested in you? What practices or habits were most impactful? What aspects of their approach are worth imitating?

If you have not had someone personally disciple you, explain that clearly and reflect on how you have grown spiritually instead. As you write, ask yourself: What helped me grow the most in my faith? What kind of investment do I wish I had received? What can I begin practicing now? What do I still need to learn in order to disciple others?

After completing your reflection, reduce your thoughts to one sentence that captures your discipleship experience. Be prepared to share how your experience shapes the way you think about discipling others moving forward.

Reflections:

One-Sentence Summary:

STRUCTURE STAGE

HOW HAS GOD WIRED YOU?

After the framing is complete, the structure begins to take shape. This is where the individual parts come together to form a functioning whole. Each beam, joint, and support has a role, and the strength of the structure depends on how those parts work together. No single piece carries the entire load, but every piece matters.

In the same way, God has not designed His people to function in isolation. He has wired each person uniquely and placed them within a body so that, together, they accomplish His purposes. This section helps you understand how you are designed and how you fit within the team.

Scripture makes it clear that the church is a body with many parts, each gifted differently but united in Christ (1 Cor. 12; Eph. 4). God gives both spiritual gifts and leadership tendencies so that His people can be equipped and built up into maturity.

In this section, you will explore *team dynamics* and *leadership dynamics*. Team dynamics will help you identify your spiritual gifts and how they contribute to the body. Leadership dynamics will help you understand how you naturally lead and relate to others within the team. Together, these lessons will help you see not only how you are built, but how you are meant to function alongside others in what God is building.

STEP 5:

TEAM DYNAMICS

1 CORINTHIANS 12:4-7, 12-14

God gives different gifts to build one unified body. In 1 Corinthians 12, Paul addresses a church struggling with comparison and confusion about spiritual gifts. His goal is to show that diversity in gifting is not a problem—it is God's design. The church is not meant to function as a collection of identical people, but as a unified body made up of distinct parts. Understanding this helps us see both our role and our need for others.

First, there are different gifts, but the same source. Paul writes, "There are varieties of gifts, but the same Spirit… varieties of service, but the same Lord" (1 Cor. 12:4–5). This means that every gift comes from God, and no gift is superior in value. Whether visible or behind the scenes, every role is given by the Spirit. This guards us from pride and insecurity. You are not responsible to be everything—you are responsible to be faithful with what God has given you. How might your mindset shift if you saw your gifts as a stewardship rather than a status?

Second, gifts are given for the good of others. Paul says, "To each is given the manifestation of the Spirit for the common good" (1 Cor. 12:7). Your gifts are not primarily for your own fulfillment—they are for the strengthening of the body. This means your role matters because others depend on it. When you use your gifts, the church is built up; when you withhold them, the church lacks something God intended it to have. This reframes how we think about participation—it is not optional, but essential. In what ways have you seen your gifts benefit others?

Third, the body needs every part. Paul explains, "For just as the body is one and has many members… so it is with Christ" (1 Cor. 12:12). He goes on to emphasize that no part can say to another, "I have no need of you" (1 Cor. 12:21). This means both that you need others and others need you. Team dynamics are not about independence, but interdependence. Healthy teams recognize differences, honor each role, and work together toward a shared mission. Where do you tend to rely on others well, and where do you struggle to do so?

As you consider team dynamics, remember that God has placed you in the body intentionally. Your gifts are needed, and so are the gifts of others. The goal is not to compare or compete, but to contribute. Understanding this helps us function as a unified team, built by God and for His purposes.

**YOU ARE NOT MEANT TO DO EVERYTHING.
YOU ARE MEANT TO DO YOUR PART.**

EXERCISE

Complete a spiritual gifts assessment, then reflect on the results (see Appendix A for an assessment). On one page, describe what you believe your spiritual gifts are and how you have seen them at work in your life. Consider specific examples where these gifts have been evident, both inside and outside the church. Also reflect on affirmations you've received from others—what have people consistently noticed or encouraged in you?

As you write, ask yourself: What do I naturally do that seems to benefit others spiritually? Where have I seen fruit? What do others affirm in me? Do the assessment results align with my experience? After completing your reflection, reduce your thoughts to one sentence that captures your primary gifting. Be prepared to share how your gifts might contribute to the team and where you may need others to complement you.

Reflections:

One-Sentence Summary:

STEP 6:

LEADERSHIP DYNAMICS

EPHESIANS 4:11-13

Christ gives different leadership expressions to equip His church for maturity. In Ephesians 4, Paul explains that Christ builds His church not by elevating a few, but by equipping all His people for the work of ministry. Every believer serves, and every believer influences others in some way. Some lead more directionally, helping guide and equip the body, while others strengthen the work through faithful support and participation. These are not positions of status, but functions within the body. Each expression contributes uniquely so that the whole church grows into maturity. Understanding these dynamics helps us see how we serve, how we influence, and how we work together as God builds His church.

First, Christ is the source of all leadership and equipping. Paul writes, "He gave the apostles, the prophets, the evangelists, the shepherds and teachers" (Eph. 4:11). These are gifts from Christ to His church, not positions of status, but ways He cares for and builds His people. Each expression reflects something of Christ's own ministry: apostles pioneer, prophets call to truth, evangelists proclaim the gospel, shepherds care for people, and teachers ground others in Scripture. No one embodies all of these fully, but each person tends to reflect one or more of them in how they serve and influence others. Which of these do you naturally gravitate toward, and why?

Second, these leadership expressions exist to equip others. Paul continues, "to equip the saints for the work of ministry" (Eph. 4:12). The goal is not for a few to do the ministry, but for all to be prepared to serve. Some may lead more directionally, helping guide and develop others, while many strengthen the work through faithful service, support, and participation. This shifts the focus from performance to empowerment. Healthy leadership multiplies itself by equipping others, not by centralizing responsibility. This means every believer is a minister. How have you seen leadership either equip others or unintentionally limit them?

Third, the goal is maturity and unity. Paul concludes, "until we all attain to the unity of the faith… to mature manhood, to the measure of the stature of the fullness of Christ" (Eph. 4:13). The aim is not control or growth in numbers alone, but spiritual maturity in the whole body. Each expression contributes differently to this goal, but all are necessary. When they work together, the church becomes stable, unified, and effective. Where do you see yourself contributing to the maturity of others, and where do you need others to strengthen you?

As you reflect on these dynamics, remember that no single person carries everything. God distributes these expressions across His people so the church can function fully. Understanding how you serve—and how others complement you—helps build a team that is both balanced and effective in ministry.

THE GOAL IS NOT FOR A FEW TO DO THE MINISTRY, BUT FOR ALL TO BE PREPARED TO SERVE.

EXERCISE

Complete an APEST assessment (see Appendix B for an assessment). Then, on one page, briefly describe each role in your own words. After that, reflect on which roles you resonate with most and least. Consider your past experiences—where have you naturally taken initiative, influenced others, or contributed to the work? Who have you worked well with, and what ways of leading and serving have energized or frustrated you?

As you write, ask yourself: Where do I tend to take initiative or influence others? What kinds of people do I work best with? What approaches to leadership or service challenge me? How has God used me to build others up? After completing your reflection, reduce your thoughts to one sentence that captures how you tend to lead and influence. Be prepared to share how your tendencies may complement others on the team and where you may need balance.

Reflections:

One-Sentence Summary:

CHALLENGE STAGE

WHAT MIGHT HOLD YOU BACK?

As the structure rises, every build encounters pressure points. No structure is assembled without tension—weight shifts, materials are tested, and weak spots are exposed. A wise builder does not ignore these realities but anticipates them, reinforcing areas that could compromise the whole.

In the same way, as God forms a people for His work, challenges will surface. Some are internal—fears, insecurities, and hesitations. Others are external—resistance, difficulty, and environments that seem hard to reach. This section helps you identify and understand those challenges so they can be faced with clarity and faith.

Scripture shows that God does not remove challenges from His people but uses them to strengthen and prepare them. From Moses' hesitation to the spiritual battles described by Paul, we see that both internal and external pressures are part of the work of ministry.

In this section, you will examine *internal fears* and *external strongholds*. Internal fears will help you uncover what may hold you back from stepping forward in obedience. External strongholds will help you recognize the spiritual realities that make certain people or places difficult to reach. Together, these lessons will help you move forward not with avoidance, but with awareness and dependence on God.

STEP 7:

INTERNAL FEARS

EXODUS 3:10-12; 4:10-12

God's calling often confronts our fears, but His presence is enough. In Exodus 3–4, God calls Moses to lead His people out of Egypt, and Moses immediately responds with hesitation and fear. This is one of the clearest pictures in Scripture of how internal fears surface when God calls someone into His work. Moses is not rebellious—he is aware of his limitations. This passage helps us see that fear is not unusual in calling, but it must be addressed in light of who God is.

First, God calls us beyond our perceived ability. The Lord says, "Come, I will send you to Pharaoh" (Ex. 3:10). This is a massive assignment, and Moses immediately feels inadequate. God's calling often stretches us beyond what feels comfortable or possible. If we only step into what we feel capable of, we will rarely depend on God. Calling exposes our limits so that we see our need for Him. When you think about what lies ahead, where do you feel most inadequate or unprepared?

Second, our fears often reveal where we trust ourselves. Moses responds, "Who am I that I should go?" (Ex. 3:11), and later, "I am not eloquent… I am slow of speech" (Ex. 4:10). His focus is on his own ability, or lack of it. Fear tends to center us on ourselves—our weaknesses, our past, our limitations. While those may be real, they are not ultimate. Fear often exposes where we are still relying on our own strength rather than trusting God's sufficiency. What do your fears say about what you believe you need in order to be effective?

Third, God answers fear with His presence. The Lord responds, "But I will be with you" (Ex. 3:12), and again, "I will be with your mouth and teach you what you shall speak" (Ex. 4:12). God does not deny Moses' weakness—He redirects his focus. The solution to fear is not increased confidence in self, but deeper trust in God's presence. This is the foundation for moving forward in obedience. You may not feel ready, but God promises to be with you. How might your fears change if you truly believed God's presence was enough?

As you reflect on your internal fears, do not try to ignore them or eliminate them on your own. Instead, bring them into the light and examine them in light of God's calling and God's presence. Fear does not disqualify you—it invites you to trust God more deeply as you step into what He is asking you to do.

FEAR REVEALS WHERE YOU ARE STILL TRUSTING YOURSELF.

EXERCISE

On one page, describe the fears you have as you think about stepping into ministry and what may be expected of you. Be honest and specific. Identify not only what you fear, but why you fear it. Then, make a short list of tasks, roles, or situations in church or ministry that you tend to avoid or dislike.

As you write, ask yourself: What am I most afraid of failing at? Where do I feel inadequate? What situations make me uncomfortable or hesitant? Why do these fears exist? After completing your reflection, reduce your thoughts to one sentence that captures your primary fear. Be prepared to share and discuss how these fears may affect your role on the team and how the group can support you in moving forward faithfully.

Reflections:

One-Sentence Summary:

STEP 8:

EXTERNAL STRONGHOLDS

2 CORINTHIANS 10:3-5

The battle in ministry is spiritual, and God has given us the weapons to overcome. In 2 Corinthians 10, Paul addresses opposition to his ministry and clarifies the nature of the fight. Though ministry happens in the real world—with people, places, and visible challenges—the true battle is not merely external. It is spiritual, rooted in thoughts, beliefs, and systems that resist the knowledge of God. This passage helps us see that what appears difficult on the surface often has deeper spiritual realities underneath.

First, we live in the world, but we do not fight like the world. Paul writes, "For though we walk in the flesh, we are not waging war according to the flesh" (2 Cor. 10:3). This means that while we engage real people and real situations, our approach cannot be purely human—strategy, personality, or effort alone are not enough. Ministry is not ultimately a social or organizational problem to solve; it is a spiritual mission to engage. Where do you tend to rely on human solutions when facing difficult people or places?

Second, God provides spiritual weapons with real power. Paul says, "The weapons of our warfare are not of the flesh but have divine power to destroy strongholds" (2 Cor.

10:4). These strongholds are not physical structures but entrenched patterns of thinking—beliefs, lies, and worldviews that resist God's truth. The power to address these does not come from us, but from God. His Word, His Spirit, and prayer are the means by which strongholds are confronted and broken. When you think about difficult environments, what deeper beliefs or patterns might be shaping them?

Third, the goal is transformation through truth. Paul explains, "We destroy arguments and every lofty opinion raised against the knowledge of God, and take every thought captive to obey Christ" (2 Cor. 10:5). The aim is not simply behavior change, but renewed thinking that leads to obedience. Strongholds are dismantled as truth replaces lies. This reminds us that ministry is not just about reaching people, but about helping them see clearly who God is and respond rightly. How might your approach to difficult people or places change if you focused on the beliefs beneath the surface?

As you consider external strongholds, begin to look beyond what is visible to what is spiritual. Difficult people, resistant environments, and challenging situations are not just obstacles—they are opportunities for God's truth to bring transformation. Understanding this helps us move forward with clarity, humility, and dependence on God's power.

THE GREATEST BARRIERS ARE OFTEN NOT VISIBLE. THEY ARE BELIEVED.

EXERCISE

On one page, list the places, people groups, or situations that seem hardest to reach with the gospel. Be specific—think about environments, communities, or relational dynamics that feel resistant or closed off. Then reflect on why these feel difficult. Consider not just surface-level challenges, but what deeper beliefs, fears, or patterns might be at work.

As you write, ask yourself: What makes this group or place feel resistant? What attitudes or beliefs might be shaping them? Where do I feel least effective or most discouraged? Why? After completing your reflection, reduce your thoughts to one sentence that captures the primary challenge you see. Be prepared to share and discuss how we might pray and think strategically about engaging these strongholds together.

Reflections:

One-Sentence Summary:

PLACEMENT STAGE

WHERE HAS GOD PLACED YOU?

Once a structure is built, it is not left in isolation—it is placed with purpose. Every structure is set within a specific location, surrounded by a particular environment, and designed to serve a function in that place. Its effectiveness is tied not only to how it is built, but to where it is placed.

In the same way, God does not form His people without intention for where they will live and serve. He places each person within a context—relationships, neighborhoods, workplaces, and communities—so that they might participate in His mission there. This section helps you see your surroundings not randomly, but strategically.

Scripture shows that God's mission unfolds in real places among real people. The apostles did not minister in abstraction—they understood cities, engaged cultures, and proclaimed the gospel in specific contexts.

In this section, you will explore *your city terrain* and your *dreams for the city*. City terrain will help you observe and understand the rhythms, needs, and opportunities around you. City dreams will help you align your vision with God's greater purpose and imagine what gospel transformation could look like. Together, these lessons will help you see not only where God has placed you, but why He has placed you there.

STEP 9:

CITY TERRAIN

ACTS 17:22-23

Effective mission begins with understanding people and place. In Acts 17, Paul arrives in Athens and does not begin by immediately preaching—he begins by observing. He studies the city, walks its streets, and pays attention to what people value. This moment shows us that faithful gospel ministry is not disconnected from context. If we are going to reach people, we must first understand where they are and how they live.

First, Paul carefully observes his surroundings. Luke notes that Paul was in the marketplace and then says, "So Paul, standing in the midst of the Areopagus, said… 'I perceive that in every way you are very religious'" (Acts 17:22). This observation did not come from assumption—it came from paying attention. Paul noticed their altars, their habits, and their patterns of life. He took time to understand before he spoke. This reminds us that mission begins with awareness, not activity. How well do you truly know the rhythms, values, and patterns of the people around you?

Second, Paul seeks to understand their beliefs and culture. He references an altar "to the unknown god" (Acts 17:23), showing that he not only saw their environment but understood what it meant. He recognized their spiritual hunger and their confusion. Paul did not ignore their culture—he engaged it thoughtfully. In the same way, our communities are shaped by beliefs, fears, desires, and assumptions that influence how people live. If we do not understand these, we will struggle to connect the gospel meaningfully. What beliefs or values seem to shape your community?

Third, Paul connects the gospel to their context. He says, "What therefore you worship as unknown, this I proclaim to you" (Acts 17:23). Paul builds a bridge from their world to the truth of God. He does not change the message, but he communicates it in a way that makes sense to them. This is the goal of understanding terrain—not just knowledge, but connection. When we understand people well, we can speak clearly and faithfully into their lives. Where do you see natural opportunities to connect the gospel to everyday life in your community?

As you think about your city or community, begin to see it not just as a place you live, but as a field you are sent into. God has placed you there intentionally. The more you understand your surroundings, the more effectively you can participate in His mission. Observation, understanding, and connection are key to faithful ministry.

MISSION BEGINS WITH OBSERVATION BEFORE PROCLAMATION.

EXERCISE

Study your community and map out what you observe. On one page (or using a digital map), identify key pathways (how people move in and out), gathering places (where people spend time), rhythms (daily or weekly patterns), and needs (both physical and spiritual). Pay attention to where people naturally congregate and what seems to matter most to them.

As you do this, ask yourself: Where do people spend their time? What do they value? What are their needs or struggles? Where are natural points of connection? Who do I already interact with, and where do those interactions happen? After mapping your observations, be prepared to share what you are seeing and how it might shape our approach to mission in this area.

Reflections:

One-Sentence Summary:

STEP 10:

CITY DREAMS

REVELATION 7:9-10

God's mission is to gather a people from every place into worship around His Son. In Revelation 7, John is given a vision of the end—the result of God's redemptive work in the world. What he sees is not a small or limited outcome, but a vast multitude from every nation, tribe, people, and language standing before the throne. This vision helps us understand that our dreams for our city are not meant to originate from us alone, but to align with what God is already doing on a global scale.

First, God's vision is expansive. John writes, "a great multitude that no one could number, from every nation" (Rev. 7:9). This shows us that God's heart is not narrow or limited—His mission reaches across every boundary. When we think about our city, we are not just thinking about a location, but about people from diverse backgrounds, stories, and needs. Our vision should reflect the breadth of God's desire to save and gather people. How might your perspective change if you saw your city as part of God's global mission?

Second, God's vision is centered on worship. The multitude is "standing before the throne and before the Lamb… crying out with a loud voice, 'Salvation belongs to our God'"

(Rev. 7:9–10). The goal is not simply changed lives, but transformed lives that worship Christ. Everything in ministry moves toward this—people seeing Jesus rightly and responding in faith. This means our dreams must go beyond surface-level improvement and aim at true spiritual transformation. When you think about your city, do your hopes center on people coming to know and worship Christ?

Third, God's vision is certain and victorious. This scene is not a possibility—it is a promise. God will accomplish His purpose. This gives us confidence to dream boldly, not because of our ability, but because of God's plan. We are not trying to build something uncertain; we are participating in something guaranteed. This frees us to think big, pray boldly, and act faithfully. What might you ask God to do in your city if you truly believed He is able and willing?

As you consider your dreams for the city, let them be shaped by this vision—expansive, centered on Christ, and grounded in confidence in God's power. Your role is not to limit what God might do, but to align your heart with His purposes and step forward in faith.

YOUR VISION SHOULD BE SHAPED BY GOD'S MISSION.

EXERCISE

On one page, describe your vision for gospel impact in your city. Think beyond what seems immediately realistic and allow yourself to imagine what God could do. Be specific—what would it look like for people to come to faith? What kinds of relationships, ministries, or movements would need to exist? What process or steps might help move toward that vision over time?

As you write, ask yourself: What do I long to see God do here? What would transformation look like in this community? Who would be reached, and how? What role might I or our team play? After completing your reflection, reduce your vision to one sentence that clearly captures your dream for the city. Be prepared to share and discuss how your vision aligns with others and how it might shape our direction moving forward.

Reflections:

....

....

....

....

....

....

....

....

....

....

....

....

....

....

....

....

....

....

....

....

One-Sentence Summary:

POWER STAGE

HOW WILL WE RELY ON GOD?

A structure may be well-built and properly placed, but without power, it remains inactive. It cannot function as intended. Power brings life to what has been built—it enables movement, usefulness, and impact.

In the same way, the Christian life and the work of ministry cannot operate on design alone. No amount of preparation, clarity, or structure can replace the need for God's power. What God builds, He also sustains. This section shifts the focus from what has been formed to how it is sustained—by dependence on God Himself.

Scripture makes it clear that the life of God's people is not fueled by human strength, but by His presence. Jesus calls His disciples to abide in Him, and promises the Holy Spirit to empower them for mission.

In this section, you will explore *depending on God* and *trusting the Spirit*. Depending on God will help you develop a life of prayer and ongoing reliance on Christ. Trusting the Spirit will help you understand how God works in and through you for His purposes. Together, these lessons will remind you that everything God builds must be sustained by Him if it is to bear lasting fruit.

STEP 11:

DEPENDING ON GOD

JOHN 15:4-5

Apart from Christ, we can do nothing of lasting value. In John 15, Jesus is preparing His disciples for life and ministry after His departure. Rather than giving them strategies or structures, He gives them a picture—a vine and branches. This image is meant to shape how they understand their relationship to Him and their ability to bear fruit. The foundation of all ministry is not activity, but dependence.

First, dependence begins with abiding in Christ. Jesus says, "Abide in me, and I in you" (Jn. 15:4). To abide means to remain, to stay connected, to live in an ongoing relationship. This is not a one-time decision but a continual posture. The branch does not occasionally connect to the vine—it lives from it. In the same way, our lives and ministry must be rooted in ongoing communion with Christ through His Word and prayer. Where in your life do you tend to drift from consistent dependence on Christ?

Second, fruitfulness flows from connection, not effort. Jesus continues, "As the branch cannot bear fruit by itself, unless it abides in the vine, neither can you" (Jn. 15:4). This is a clear statement: effort alone cannot produce spiritual fruit. We can be busy, organized, and even effective in human terms, but without abiding in Christ, it will not result in lasting spiritual impact. True fruit—transformed lives, genuine discipleship, lasting change—comes from connection to Him. How might your approach to ministry change if you focused more on connection than activity?

Third, separation from Christ results in nothing. Jesus makes it unmistakable: "Apart from me you can do nothing" (Jn. 15:5). This is not a partial limitation—it is a complete one. Without Christ, we may accomplish things, but they will lack eternal value. This humbles us and redirects us. Dependence is not weakness—it is the pathway to effectiveness. The more we recognize our need for Christ, the more we position ourselves for Him to work through us. What areas of your life or ministry reveal a lack of dependence on Christ?

As you reflect on depending on God, remember that prayer is not an accessory to ministry—it is the lifeline of it. Abiding in Christ shapes everything else. Before we act, we must remain. Before we lead, we must depend. This is how fruit is produced in the life of a believer and in the life of a church.

APART FROM CHRIST, NOTHING OF LASTING VALUE IS PRODUCED.

EXERCISE

For one week, commit to intentionally praying for a specific group of people or a particular place in your community. Set aside consistent time each day to pray, asking God to work in their lives and to give you insight, compassion, and opportunity. Keep a record of your prayers and any thoughts, impressions, or ideas that come as you pray.

As you go through the week, ask yourself: How is God shaping my heart toward these people? What am I beginning to notice that I didn't before? What opportunities might God be opening? How is my dependence on Him growing? At the end of the week, be prepared to share what you experienced—both in your prayer life and in your perspective—and how God may be leading you to act moving forward.

Reflections:

One-Sentence Summary:

STEP 12:

TRUSTING THE SPIRIT

ACTS 1:8

The Holy Spirit empowers believers to live and witness beyond their natural ability. In Acts 1, Jesus is preparing His disciples for His ascension. They are about to step into the mission without His physical presence, and instead of giving them a strategy, He gives them a promise—the Holy Spirit. This moment is critical because it shows that the success of their mission will not depend on their strength, but on God's power at work within them.

First, the Spirit provides power for what God calls us to do. Jesus says, "You will receive power when the Holy Spirit has come upon you" (Acts 1:8). The disciples were not ready in themselves to carry out the mission, but God did not expect them to be. The Spirit supplies what we lack—boldness, wisdom, endurance, and effectiveness. This means we do not have to rely on our personality, experience, or confidence alone. God meets us with His power. Where do you feel most aware of your need for God's power in your life or ministry?

Second, the Spirit empowers us for witness. Jesus continues, "and you will be my witnesses" (Acts 1:8). The purpose of the Spirit's power is not personal experience alone—it is *mission*. The Spirit enables us to speak, live, and represent Christ in a way that points others to Him. This includes both our words and our lives. The Spirit works through ordinary people to make Christ known. How might your understanding of the Holy Spirit change if you saw His primary role as empowering you for mission?

Third, the Spirit expands the scope of our mission. Jesus outlines the progression: "in Jerusalem and in all Judea and Samaria, and to the end of the earth" (Acts 1:8). The Spirit not only empowers the mission but also extends it beyond what we would naturally pursue. The disciples would move from what was familiar to what was uncomfortable and even difficult. The same is true for us—trusting the Spirit often leads us beyond our comfort zones into places where we must depend on Him more deeply. Where might the Spirit be leading you beyond what feels natural or comfortable?

As you consider trusting the Spirit, remember that He is not distant or abstract—He is actively at work in and through you. The Christian life is not meant to be lived in your own strength. The Spirit empowers, guides, and sustains you for the mission of God. Learning to trust Him means stepping forward in faith, even when you feel inadequate, knowing that God is at work within you.

THE SPIRIT EMPOWERS ORDINARY PEOPLE FOR EXTRAORDINARY MISSION.

EXERCISE

Write a paragraph describing your most meaningful or powerful experience with the Holy Spirit. This could be a moment of conviction, guidance, boldness, comfort, or clarity —any time when you were especially aware of God's presence and work in your life.

After that, reflect on the following questions: What made that experience impactful? What conditions were present in your life at the time (such as prayer, surrender, obedience, or need)? How did it affect your relationship with God? In what ways did it change your perspective or actions? What might it look like to pursue a deeper dependence on the Spirit moving forward?

Be prepared to share both your experience and your reflections, considering how the Spirit has worked in your life and how you can remain open and responsive to His leading in the future.

Reflections:

One-Sentence Summary:

CONCLUSION

God is building His church, and He builds it through people. What you have worked through in this guide is a process of stepping back to see the blueprint of your life more clearly. Piece by piece, you have traced the foundation God has laid, examined the framework He has formed through your experiences, identified how He has structured you through your gifts, faced the challenges that must be strengthened, considered where He has placed you, and been reminded that all of it depends on His power.

Like any structure, much of what matters most is not immediately visible. Foundations are buried. Frameworks are covered. Reinforcements are hidden. Yet these are the very things that determine whether something will stand. In the same way, the work God has done—and continues to do—in you is often unseen, but it is essential. He has been forming you with intention, shaping your life through every season, every relationship, and every experience. Nothing has been wasted. Everything has been part of His design.

At the same time, this process has not been about you alone. God does not build isolated structures—He builds a people. Throughout this journey, you have begun to see not only how you are designed, but how you fit with others. Different gifts, different experiences, different callings—all brought together by God to form something stronger and more complete than any one person could be on their own. This is how Christ builds His church: by forming individuals and placing them together for His purposes.

As you move forward, remember that this is not the end of formation, but the beginning of clarity. The blueprint is clearer, but the building continues. There will be new challenges to strengthen, new opportunities to step into, and deeper dependence required along the way. What matters is that you continue to trust the Builder. He is faithful. He knows what He is doing. And He is committed to completing what He has started.

So walk forward with confidence—not in yourself, but in Him. You are not building alone. The Builder is at work, forming you and placing you exactly where you are needed.

APPENDIX A:

GIFT ASSESSMENT

God has not only saved His people—He has equipped them. Every believer is given spiritual gifts for the purpose of building up the church and advancing His mission. These gifts are not random abilities, but intentional expressions of God's grace at work through His people.

This gift assessment is designed to help you identify and understand how God has uniquely gifted you. The goal is not to label you, but to help you recognize how you serve, strengthen, and contribute to the body of Christ. As with leadership dynamics, these gifts are best understood in community and confirmed through faithful service. Here is a brief explanation of each:

Teaching – The Instructor. Explains and applies Scripture clearly so others can understand truth and grow in obedience.

Shepherding – The Caregiver. Cares for and guides others spiritually, helping them grow through consistent, relational investment.

Evangelism – The Witness. Communicates the gospel naturally and clearly, helping others take steps toward faith in Christ.

Leadership – The Organizer. Provides direction, organizes people and efforts, and helps move a group toward a shared goal.

Service – The Helper. Recognizes and meets practical needs with humility, often working behind the scenes.

Encouragement – The Strengthener. Builds others up through timely words, presence, and support, helping them stay motivated and faithful.

Giving – The Contributor. Generously and joyfully shares resources to support God's work and meet the needs of others.

Faith – The Truster. Trusts God deeply in uncertain situations and inspires others to rely on Him with confidence.

This assessment focuses on core, observable gifts that strengthen a missional team. Other gifts in Scripture are not excluded, but are reflected here or better understood through experience and maturity. Some categories, such as teaching, shepherding, and evangelism, also appear in the APEST framework—there they describe leadership tendencies, while here they describe how individuals serve. Not everyone who has a gift will lead in that area, but every gift contributes to the strength of the team.

HOW TO TAKE THE ASSESSMENT

Read each statement carefully and evaluate how true it is of you. For each statement, assign a score using the scale below. Once you have completed all the statements, add your totals for each gift. Then, identify your highest two or three scores, as these will indicate your strongest areas of contribution within the team.

1 = Not true of me
2 = Slightly true of me
3 = Somewhat true of me
4 = Mostly true of me
5 = Very true of me

INTERPRETING THE RESULTS

Your results are not a label—they are a starting point. They reveal how you serve, not your limits, and should be confirmed through Scripture, experience, and the affirmation of others. Use this as a tool for reflection and discussion, not a final definition of who you are. Just as every structure requires different components to stand, every team depends on a variety of gifts working together, and God builds His church through a unified body.

TEACHING (THE INSTRUCTOR)

Those with this gift seek to understand Scripture deeply, explain truth clearly, and help others grow in knowledge and obedience.

________ I enjoy studying Scripture in order to understand it deeply.

________ I can explain biblical truth in a way others understand.

________ I am drawn to helping others grow in knowledge of God's Word.

________ I notice when teaching lacks clarity or accuracy.

________ I often organize ideas to make them easier to understand.

________ I enjoy answering questions about Scripture.

________ I am motivated to ensure truth is communicated correctly.

________ I find fulfillment when others grow in understanding.

________ I regularly reflect on how Scripture applies to life.

________ I prefer depth of understanding over surface-level discussion.

________ I often help others think more clearly about spiritual matters.

________ I feel responsible to help others understand truth rightly.

________ **SCORE**

SHEPHERDING (THE CAREGIVER)

Those with this gift care for people relationally, guiding and nurturing others toward spiritual growth over time.

________ I care deeply about the spiritual health of others.

________ I am drawn to walk with people through life's challenges.

________ I notice when someone is struggling or disconnected.

________ I value meaningful relationships over tasks.

________ I am willing to invest in people over long periods of time.

________ People often come to me for personal guidance.

________ I feel a responsibility to help others grow spiritually.

________ I am burdened when people are neglected or overlooked.

________ I think about how decisions affect people personally.

________ I want others to feel known and cared for.

________ I am patient with people as they grow.

________ I am motivated to help people remain connected to the church.

________ **SCORE**

EVANGELISM (THE WITNESS)

Those with this gift communicate the gospel naturally, connect with others easily, and are motivated to see people come to faith in Christ.

________ I look for opportunities to share my faith.

________ I feel a burden for those who do not know Christ.

________ I am comfortable starting conversations with new people.

________ I enjoy connecting with people outside the church.

________ I often think about how to communicate the gospel clearly.

________ I am energized when people respond to the gospel.

________ I naturally bring spiritual topics into conversation.

________ I want others to grow in confidence to share their faith.

________ I am drawn toward people who are far from God.

________ I am willing to take initiative in outreach situations.

________ I think about how to make the gospel accessible to others.

________ I am burdened when the church loses focus on reaching others.

________ **SCORE**

LEADERSHIP (THE ORGANIZER)

Those with this gift provide direction, organize people and efforts, and help groups move forward toward a shared purpose.

________ I naturally take initiative in group settings.

________ I can organize people and resources toward a goal.

________ Others often look to me for direction.

________ I enjoy helping groups move forward with clarity.

________ I think strategically about how to accomplish tasks.

________ I am comfortable making decisions when needed.

________ I can see what needs to be done and how to do it.

________ I help others stay focused and aligned.

________ I enjoy bringing structure to unclear situations.

________ I am motivated to help a group succeed together.

________ I take responsibility when leadership is needed.

________ I think about how to improve systems and processes.

________ **SCORE**

SERVICE (THE HELPER)

Those with this gift recognize practical needs and meet them faithfully, often working behind the scenes to support others.

________ I enjoy meeting practical needs behind the scenes.

________ I often notice what needs to be done before others do.

________ I take action without needing recognition.

________ I find fulfillment in helping others succeed.

________ I am willing to do tasks others may overlook.

________ I prefer serving over leading publicly.

________ I am dependable in completing necessary tasks.

________ I support others so they can focus on their roles.

________ I am motivated by seeing needs met.

________ I am consistent in helping where needed.

________ I enjoy contributing in practical ways.

________ I do not need attention to feel valued in my work.

________ **SCORE**

ENCOURAGEMENT (THE STRENGTHENER)

Those with this gift build others up through words, presence, and support, helping people remain encouraged and faithful.

________ I regularly speak words that uplift others.

________ I am drawn to people who are discouraged.

________ I help others see hope in difficult situations.

________ People feel strengthened after talking with me.

________ I naturally affirm others' growth and potential.

________ I enjoy helping others stay motivated.

________ I speak truth in a way that builds others up.

________ I help people move forward when they feel stuck.

________ I am sensitive to emotional and spiritual needs.

________ I want others to remain faithful and encouraged.

________ I look for opportunities to strengthen others.

________ I help create a positive and supportive environment.

________ **SCORE**

GIVING (THE CONTRIBUTOR)

Those with this gift give generously and joyfully, using their resources to support God's work and meet the needs of others.

________ I am eager to give my resources to meet needs.

________ I think intentionally about supporting God's work financially.

________ I give generously and with joy.

________ I look for opportunities to provide for others.

________ I see my resources as tools for ministry.

________ I am willing to sacrifice in order to give.

________ I am motivated to support meaningful work.

________ I give without needing recognition.

________ I enjoy helping meet tangible needs.

________ I feel fulfillment when others are provided for.

________ I manage my resources with generosity in mind.

________ I want my giving to make an impact.

________ **SCORE**

FAITH (THE TRUSTER)

Those with this gift trust God deeply, remain steady in uncertainty, and inspire others to rely on Him with confidence.

________ I trust God even when circumstances are uncertain.

________ I believe God will act in difficult situations.

________ I remain hopeful when others feel discouraged.

________ I encourage others to trust God more deeply.

________ I rely on God rather than my own understanding.

________ I have confidence in God's promises.

________ I remain steady in challenging situations.

________ I believe God can do what seems unlikely.

________ I help others see God's faithfulncss.

________ I am not easily shaken by uncertainty.

________ I look to God first in difficult situations.

________ I am confident in God's ability to provide and lead.

________ **SCORE**

APPENDIX B:

APEST ASSESSMENT

Leadership within the church is not one-size-fits-all. Scripture shows that Christ equips His people through different leadership expressions (Eph. 4:11–13). This framework (sometimes called APEST) helps us understand five ways believers influence and serve: Apostle, Prophet, Evangelist, Shepherd, and Teacher. Some express these more directionally, but all reflect them in how they contribute to the team.

Apostle (A) – The Builder. Apostles are pioneers who think in terms of mission, movement, and expansion. They are drawn to starting new works, organizing people, and building systems that advance the gospel.

Prophet (P) – The Guardian. Prophets are driven by truth and alignment with God's Word. They discern what is right or wrong and call people to faithfulness, often challenging compromise.

Evangelist (E) – The Messenger. Evangelists are passionate about reaching people with the gospel. They connect easily with others and are energized by seeing people take steps toward faith in Christ.

Shepherd (S) – The Caregiver. Shepherds care for people relationally. They nurture, guide, and support others, helping them grow spiritually and remain connected to the body.

Teacher (T) – The Clarifier. Teachers are committed to understanding and explaining Scripture. They bring clarity and stability by helping others grasp and apply truth.

HOW TO TAKE THE ASSESSMENT

Read each statement carefully and evaluate how true it is of you. For each statement, assign a score using the scale below. Once you have completed all the statements, add your totals for each category (A, P, E, S, T). Then, identify your highest and second-highest scores, as these will indicate your strongest leadership tendencies.

1 = Not true of me

2 = Slightly true of me

3 = Somewhat true of me

4 = Mostly true of me

5 = Very true of me

INTERPRETING THE RESULTS

Your results are not a label—they are a starting point. They reveal tendencies, not limits, and should be confirmed through Scripture, experience, and the affirmation of others. Use this as a tool for reflection and discussion, not a final definition of who you are. Just as every structure requires different components to stand, every team requires different leadership expressions to function, and God builds His church through a unified body working together.

APOSTLE (A) – THE BUILDER / PIONEER

Apostolic leaders tend to think missionally, build new works, organize movement, and push outward.

________ I am energized by starting new works rather than maintaining existing ones.

________ I naturally think about the bigger picture and future direction of a ministry.

________ I am drawn to build systems, structures, or strategies that help people move toward a mission.

________ I often see possibilities where others mainly see obstacles.

________ I am willing to take initiative in uncertain environments.

________ I enjoy gathering people around a vision and helping them move toward it.

________ I am restless when a ministry becomes inward-focused or stagnant.

________ I tend to think about expansion, multiplication, and long-term impact.

________ I am comfortable entering unfamiliar spaces in order to help establish something new.

________ I often ask, "What needs to be built next?"

________ I am drawn to leadership that creates movement, not just maintenance.

________ I can usually identify what needs to change in order for a mission to advance.

________ **SCORE**

PROPHET (P) – THE GUARDIAN

Prophetic leaders tend to value truth, holiness, discernment, and spiritual alignment.

________ I feel a strong burden for God's people to remain faithful to His Word.

________ I am often aware when something feels spiritually off, even if others do not notice it.

________ I am willing to speak hard truths when necessary.

________ I care deeply about integrity, holiness, and faithfulness.

________ I am sensitive to compromise or drift in people or ministries.

________ I often feel compelled to call people back to what is right.

________ I value honesty and clarity more than comfort or appearance.

________ I am burdened when truth is neglected, watered down, or ignored.

________ I often discern underlying issues beneath what is visible on the surface.

________ I am drawn to confront falsehood, confusion, or misplaced priorities.

________ I care deeply that people not merely succeed outwardly, but live rightly before God.

________ I am more concerned with faithfulness than popularity.

________ **SCORE**

EVANGELIST (E) – THE MESSENGER

Evangelistic leaders tend to reach outward, connect with people, and draw others toward Christ.

________ I naturally look for opportunities to talk with others about spiritual matters.

________ I feel a strong burden for people who do not know Christ.

________ I am energized by meeting new people and building connections.

________ I often think about how to make the gospel clear and accessible to outsiders.

________ I am willing to initiate conversations with people I do not know well.

________ I feel joy when people take steps toward Christ.

________ I tend to notice those who are far from God more quickly than others do.

________ I am motivated to help the church keep an outward focus.

________ I am comfortable inviting others into Christian community or gospel conversation.

________ I often think about how to engage people beyond the walls of the church.

________ I want believers to grow in confidence for sharing their faith.

________ I am burdened when a ministry becomes disconnected from unbelievers.

________ **SCORE**

SHEPHERD (S) – THE CAREGIVER

Shepherding leaders tend to nurture people, protect relationships, and help others grow steadily.

________ I care deeply about the spiritual and emotional well-being of others.

________ I am drawn to walk with people through difficulty, growth, and healing.

________ I often notice when someone feels overlooked, discouraged, or disconnected.

________ I value relational health and unity within a group.

________ I am willing to invest patiently in people over time.

________ People often come to me when they need guidance, care, or support.

________ I feel responsible to help others mature in Christ.

________ I am burdened when people are neglected, isolated, or spiritually vulnerable.

________ I naturally think about how decisions will affect people personally.

________ I want others to feel known, loved, and cared for in the church.

________ I am drawn more to people-development than platform ministry.

________ I often ask, "Who needs care, support, or encouragement right now?"

________ **SCORE**

TEACHER (T) – THE CLARIFIER

Teaching leaders tend to seek understanding, explain truth clearly, and help others grow in biblical depth.

________ I enjoy studying Scripture carefully and understanding it accurately.

________ I want truth to be communicated clearly and faithfully.

________ I am energized by helping others understand biblical ideas.

________ I often notice when teaching is unclear, shallow, or imprecise.

________ I enjoy organizing ideas in a way that makes them easier to grasp.

________ I am burdened when people lack a solid foundation in God's Word.

________ I want others to grow not just in enthusiasm, but in understanding.

________ I often ask questions that bring clarity and precision.

________ I enjoy explaining truth in ways that lead to conviction and obedience.

________ I am drawn to instruction, learning, and theological depth.

________ I find satisfaction in helping others make sense of Scripture.

________ I care deeply that teaching be both true and useful.

________ **SCORE**

ABOUT THE AUTHOR

Jacob Abshire is a pastor, teacher, and church planter with a deep passion for forming disciples and building healthy churches. His ministry is centered on a simple conviction: that God builds His church through devoted people who are grounded in His Word, committed to one another, and dependent on His presence.

Over the years, Jacob has served in a variety of ministry contexts, helping individuals and teams grow in their understanding of Scripture and their role in God's mission. His approach to leadership development is both theological and practical—aimed not merely at transferring knowledge, but at shaping lives. He is especially passionate about equipping ordinary believers to live as disciple-makers in their everyday environments.

Jacob is a founder of Devo Church, where he seeks to cultivate a people fully devoted to Jesus and deployed for gospel impact wherever God has placed them. His work emphasizes simplicity, relational depth, and clarity of mission, helping churches avoid unnecessary complexity and focus on what matters most.

In addition to his pastoral work, Jacob creates resources (JacobAbshire.com) to serve the broader church, including writing, teaching, and developing tools that help believers grow in their faith and effectiveness. His desire is to see leaders formed—not just informed—so that they can faithfully participate in the work God is doing in the world.

www.ingramcontent.com/pod-product-compliance
Lightning Source LLC
LaVergne TN
LVHW010840120826
845149LV00017B/3330

* 9 7 8 0 9 9 6 9 7 1 6 9 0 *